AFTER HIGH SCHOOL

2019 Edition

by Brian Harris, B.A., M. Ed.

A Guide To Help You
Plan Your Future After High School

ISBN 9781791611682

CGS COMMUNICATIONS, INC.

www.cgscommunications.com

TABLE OF CONTENTS

If it is to be,
it is up to me!

INTRODUCTION

In a rapidly changing world, the career that you might be choosing in the future might be quite different than those that were available in the past. In an attempt to keep *After High School* as current as possible, it is going to be revised each year so that the career lists in this book and any other content can be updated annually to reflect current trends in society and the workplace.

Do you ever wonder what you are going to do after you finish high school? Do you sometimes wonder whether you should go to college or university, or take some other type of educational/ training program after high school? And, if you decide to go to college or university, do you sometimes wonder what program you will take? Do you sometimes worry that you might take the wrong program and waste all the money it costs to attend college or university? If you answered YES to any of these questions, you are not alone. In research I have conducted with thousands of high school students, the number one cause of stress identified by many students was related to what they were going to do when they completed high school. In more than twenty years working as a high school guidance counselor in helping high school students plan their future, I have seen many students reduce this stress and be more successful by using some of the strategies provided in this book.

Rob was a grade 11 student who spent so much time worrying about what he was going to do after high school that he was barely passing his high school courses. He couldn't decide whether he wanted to go to college or do something else because he had no idea what he would study if he went. There were days when he wondered if he would even have the marks to get accepted into any kind of educational program after high school. With the completion of activities similar to those you will find in this book, Rob was able to identify his strengths. Once he understood that the best way to plan his future was to build on these strengths he was able to identify a

Do you sometimes worry about what you are going to do when you finish high school?

Once you discover a focus for your future, you will experience greater success in all that you do.

program that best matched his interests, abilities and values. Remarkably, once he set a goal for his future, his marks in high school dramatically increased. By the end of grade 11, his course marks had increased by almost 25%, and in grade 12 his course marks increased another 8%. Rob graduated from high school and entered a college program that he loved. After graduating from college, he found a job that provided great satisfaction for him (and once again matched his interests, abilities and values).

As you think about your future, one of the most important things for you to realize is that you have to take responsibility for yourself. Some people go through life thinking that the world owes them a job, or even owes them happiness. Unfortunately for these people, they will find discouragement and a lack of fulfillment throughout their lives. They will spend much of their time blaming others (including bosses, family, friends, and even the government) for their failures without realizing that they are their own problem. The person most responsible for the life you live is you.

Jasmine was a grade 12 student who experienced problems with her parents. Whenever she did poorly in school or whenever she had a fight with her friends, she would always shrug and say to herself, "Nothing ever goes right at home so why should I expect school to be any different?" A person like Jasmine could go through her entire life blaming others for her lack of success in whatever she does. In the end, Jasmine will always get exactly what she thinks she is going to get. If she sees herself as a failure, she will always be a failure. Eventually, we all become the kind of person that we see in our minds every day.

Success begins when you take 100% responsibility for your life. It has often been said that people who have a habit of making excuses are those who struggle the most with finding happiness and success. When things aren't going the way you would like them to be going, the first person to look at is yourself. Even when negative things happen to you that you have no control over, you can still decide how you will react to what has happened. A positive person will see obstacles and setbacks as temporary problems and will seek ways to overcome them.

AFTER HIGH SCHOOL gives you an opportunity to start to plan your future. As you begin to set some goals related to your interests, abilities and values, develop a picture in your mind of being successful in achieving these goals. Every day, visualize yourself achieving your goals. As you do this, you will find yourself beginning to complete what you need to do to be successful.

AFTER HIGH SCHOOL can assist you as you attempt to plan your future education/training. Your results will also help you to better understand which careers might be best for you. For most students the right career is not just one magical job. There are generally several occupations within a field that best match your interests, abilities and values. Later in this book you will see how your interests, abilities and values can correspond to groups of "related careers." Understanding the concept of related careers within career fields can not only help you find the best job after you graduate from your future education/training, but at some point if you find yourself unemployed (or underemployed), understanding this concept can help you to find your best occupation once again.

It is recommended that you take your time and think carefully as you complete this book. Don't attempt to complete the material in this book in one evening. After each chapter, take a day or two to think about what you have done. It is also recommended that you share your results with your high school counselor/advisor and others who know you well, including your parents.

Chapter 1 gives you the opportunity to explore your interests as they relate to your experiences at high school. This chapter will also help you to form a beginning list of possible future career choices although you will explore the appropriateness of this list throughout the book. Whatever you love to do in high school (or as an interest when you are out of school) should be explored as a possibility for your future education/training. A basic theme throughout this book is that building on your strengths is one of the best approaches to achieving success in your life.

Chapter 2 explores your abilities. Most students will find that their interests and abilities go hand in hand, but if you become

Eventually, you will become the kind of person you see yourself as being.

It is more important to know where you are going than it is to get there quickly.

aware that the things that you are most interested in are different than what you do well, then this is an important area to resolve before you can successfully plan your future.

Chapter 3 will help you to identify your values and understand their importance in planning your future. Although some of our values can change over time, understanding what is important to you in your relationship with others and in your future job can help you to choose a career that will be more satisfying for you. In addition, your values influence the lifestyle you would like to have which is also impacted by your future career choice.

Chapter 4 will help you to identify a future plan after high school based on your interests, abilities and values. It has often been said that the best approach for your future is to build on your strengths. When you better understand your strengths, you will be able to choose a career that matches these strengths. When this occurs you will likely be happier in your career choice and feel satisfied in what you are doing each day at work.

Chapter 5 will help you to better understand how to achieve your goals. Dreaming about having a great future is not the same as actually doing something about it. A dream is still just a dream until you take action. Chapter 5 will provide you with some strategies that others have successfully used in attaining their dreams.

Although the first few chapters of this book can help you to better understand how your future career choice is related to your interests, abilities and values, it is important to realize that many high school students will successfully plan their immediate future after high school without knowing the exact occupation they will some day pursue. There will be more thoughts on this throughout the book.

It is okay not to know what you want to do after high school. If this book helps you to better understand your strengths and this in turn helps you to select a program at a college, university, or some other form of education or training after high school, then this is a great start.

A significant number of high school students have no idea what their future career will be when they graduate from high school, but when they are able to identify an educational/training program after high school that best matches their interests, abilities, and values, they will have taken an important first step towards future success.

Sometimes the most important first step is understanding more about you. The first chapter in this book can help you to identify your interests, an important part of identifying your strengths.

Let's get started.

Any form of work
is far more enjoyable
when you are doing
something that you
are interested in.

IDENTIFYING YOUR INTERESTS

For many years, Kelly planned to become a nurse after high school. She chose the high school courses she needed to enter a college program and worked very hard to obtain the required marks to ensure she would be admitted into the program. She held several part-time jobs to save some money to help pay for her future education. As Kelly left high school at the end of the school year, she was thrilled that she would soon be pursuing her dreams in nursing.

Ten months later I was walking through a local shopping mall and discovered Kelly selling clothes in a retail store. When I asked her how college was going, she said that she had dropped out. I immediately wondered how someone who seemed to be so set in her future plans could have experienced disappointment so quickly.

After a brief conversation with Kelly, I found out three things:

1) she strongly disliked some of the courses that were a part of her nursing program.

2) she realized her heart was not set on nursing as much as she thought it was, and that her determination for many years to become a nurse was really based on the dreams of others for her and not necessarily her own.

3) what she really loved to do was write, but she had never given this serious thought in planning her future.

Unfortunately, Kelly's story is not unusual. For some students, once they find they have made a wrong decision in their future education/training, it is often then too expensive to begin again. Many of these students complete the program they are in (and then face a career they really don't want) or drop out of their educational or

The most successful people love what they do and do what they love.

training program. How can you prevent this from happening to you?

The best answer to this question is to carefully consider what you love to do (and can do very well!) and then plan your future education/training based on this strength.

In this first chapter of *AFTER HIGH SCHOOL*, you will begin to explore your interests. What are the things that you are most interested in? What do you like to talk about?   What do you like to do? What things do you get excited about?

There is a tendency for all of us to move towards whatever we picture in our minds. We become what we think about the most, whether this is good for us or not. Unsuccessful people (and those who are miserable) often blame others for their failures, yet it is often this very picture of being unsuccessful that is locked into their minds that prevents them from becoming successful. Change what you think about and you can change your life.

This first chapter can help you to focus on your interests, and use this as a basis for thinking about your future in a manner that will help you to be more successful.

As you create a clearer picture in your mind as to what you love to do and what you do well (as explored further in the next chapter), you can begin to create an image of your future. Create a positive image of being successful in whatever you decide to do and you will begin to move towards it.

Your first step in being successful is for you to identify your dream. The first three chapters of this book can help you to crystallize a vision for your future. They can also help you to better understand whether your dream is realistic for you. And for those who still struggle with identifying a future dream after completing the first three chapters of this book, your dream for now might simply be to be the best person you can be and do the best you can do in all aspects of high school. Sometimes when we find it difficult to picture a future dream, we can still take a big step towards achieving this unknown dream by being the best we can be now in all that we do.

You can create a blueprint for your life. In working with high school students, I often found students who were worried about their future because they had no idea what they wanted to do with their life. Perhaps you are like this and that is why you are reading this book. In this chapter as you explore your interests, you will be taking your first step towards successfully planning your future after high school.

You will have the opportunity to identify your interests by choosing answers to a series of questions. It is important that you answer each question by selecting the response that is best for you. If you choose answers that are based on what you think others expect of you, you might find yourself like Kelly in a post-secondary program that becomes unbearable. Once you identify your interests, you will have taken the first step towards creating a plan for your future that will lead to a career that is satisfying for you.

There is no time limit on completing the questions in this chapter so sit back, take your time and carefully think about each of your responses. Your answers to these questions will help you to identify your interests. After doing this, you will learn which careers best match your interests.

INSTRUCTIONS: *In PART A (pages 14 - 17), answer YES or NO to each of the statements given. You must choose YES or NO for each question. In PART B (pages 18 - 22), select two statements from each group of eight. It is important that you select two statements for each group.*

Further instructions will be provided on page 23 - 26 to help you understand how your interests relate to future planning.

Sometimes when we find it difficult to picture a future dream, we can still take a big step towards achieving this unknown dream by being the best we can be now in all that we do.

IDENTIFYING YOUR INTERESTS - PART A

Do you enjoy, or do you think you would enjoy ...

1	researching important historical events	YES	NO	1
2	learning how to invest in the stock market	YES	NO	2
3	sketching pictures	YES	NO	3
4	solving mathematical problems	YES	NO	4
5	helping to coach a sports team	YES	NO	5
6	learning about scientific theories	YES	NO	6
7	achieving a high level of proficiency on a musical instrument or voice	YES	NO	7
8	making a class presentation speaking in a language other than English	YES	NO	8
9	writing code for a new software application	YES	NO	9
10	writing a creative story	YES	NO	10
11	working as a volunteer to help others in your community	YES	NO	11
12	working with machinery or power tools	YES	NO	12
13	analyzing a dramatic performance	YES	NO	13
14	learning about ancient civilizations	YES	NO	14
15	starting your own business	YES	NO	15
16	experimenting with different techniques for painting a picture	YES	NO	16
17	graphing equations	YES	NO	17
18	learning about new advances in exercise techniques	YES	NO	18
19	conducting experiments in biology	YES	NO	19
20	performing on a musical instrument or voice before a large audience	YES	NO	20
21	translating newspaper articles from one language to another	YES	NO	21
22	administering a website	YES	NO	22
23	studying the content and style of great literary works	YES	NO	23
24	helping as a teaching assistant in one of your classes	YES	NO	24
25	using a software program to design a house	YES	NO	25
26	practicing improvisation and role playing in a drama class	YES	NO	26
27	completing a project on urban planning	YES	NO	27
28	learning advertising techniques for marketing new products	YES	NO	28

Do you enjoy, or do you think you would enjoy ...

29	researching a project on the life of a famous artist	YES	NO	29
30	employing exponential functions to model real world solutions	YES	NO	30
31	researching the mechanics of human body movements	YES	NO	31
32	completing a project on an ecosystem	YES	NO	32
33	studying musical theory	YES	NO	33
34	writing an essay using a language other than your first language	YES	NO	34
35	installing security features for a home computer	YES	NO	35
36	writing articles for a magazine or newspaper	YES	NO	36
37	studying the psychology of human behavior	YES	NO	37
38	completing an electronics project	YES	NO	38
39	auditioning for a part in a local theatre presentation	YES	NO	39
40	researching different cultures	YES	NO	40
41	completing an accounting assignment.	YES	NO	41
42	analyzing the painting techniques of famous works of art	YES	NO	42
43	solving algebraic equations	YES	NO	43
44	completing a project related to nutrition	YES	NO	44
45	conducting chemistry experiments	YES	NO	45
46	practicing a musical instrument or voice for at least 1 hour every day	YES	NO	46
47	reading a novel in a language other than your first language	YES	NO	47
48	editing a video	YES	NO	48
49	discussing books you have read	YES	NO	49
50	tutoring a student who has a learning problem	YES	NO	50
51	repairing an engine	YES	NO	51
52	researching a project on contemporary theatre	YES	NO	52
53	presenting a project on solutions to environmental problems	YES	NO	53
54	reading about the rights of employees in the workplace	YES	NO	54
55	sculpting a face using clay	YES	NO	55
56	solving problems related to financial applications	YES	NO	56
57	organizing and running a house league tournament	YES	NO	57
58	learning about quantum physics	YES	NO	58

59	composing music	YES	NO	59
60	learning the vocabulary of a language other than your first language	YES	NO	60
61	designing a website for a business	YES	NO	61
62	studying the works of famous authors such as Shakespeare	YES	NO	62
63	working as a volunteer in a local hospital	YES	NO	63
64	assisting in building a house	YES	NO	64
65	creating and presenting a dramatic short play	YES	NO	65
66	exploring different political systems	YES	NO	66
67	completing a project on factors that affect our economy	YES	NO	67
68	drawing or painting copies of famous works of art	YES	NO	68
69	exploring applications of compound interest to financial investments	YES	NO	69
70	studying the psychology of being a champion athlete	YES	NO	70
71	reading about advances in microbiology	YES	NO	71
72	researching the lives of famous composers	YES	NO	72
73	interpreting someone speaking a foreign language you have learned	YES	NO	73
74	installing and configuring computer components	YES	NO	74
75	making a presentation to your class on a book you have read	YES	NO	75
76	learning the components of being an effective listener	YES	NO	76
77	helping to build a broadcast studio	YES	NO	77
78	studying set designs for plays from different historical periods	YES	NO	78
79	writing an essay on the causes of a major war	YES	NO	79
80	reading about people who have achieved great success in a business	YES	NO	80
81	completing a graphic design assignment using a computer	YES	NO	81
82	completing a project on logarithmic functions	YES	NO	82
83	working as an instructor in a fitness club	YES	NO	83
84	completing a project on the human immune system	YES	NO	84
85	providing music lessons to younger students	YES	NO	85
86	learning the grammatical rules of a foreign language	YES	NO	86
87	setting up e-commerce capabilities on a business website	YES	NO	87
88	presenting a speech on a topic of your choice	YES	NO	88

89	assisting elderly people	YES	NO	89
90	completing a course in welding	YES	NO	90
91	analyzing a dramatic play	YES	NO	91
92	reading about solutions to help resolve world hunger	YES	NO	92
93	learning about e-commerce trends	YES	NO	93
94	experimenting with light and contrast in creating designs	YES	NO	94
95	solving problems involving vectors in 2 + 3 dimensional space	YES	NO	95
96	completing a project on living a healthy lifestyle	YES	NO	96
97	learning about molecular genetics	YES	NO	97
98	using a computer to arrange a musical selection	YES	NO	98
99	studying a short story in another language you have learned	YES	NO	99
100	writing computer programs to drive devices such as robots	YES	NO	100
101	writing a fictional book	YES	NO	101
102	researching a project on the changing structure of families	YES	NO	102
103	installing mechanical devices	YES	NO	103
104	creating an original screenplay	YES	NO	104

*Congratulations on finishing **PART A**.*
*Take a break before you begin **PART B**.*
*After you complete **PART B**,*
you will be given further instructions
on how to interpret your results.

IDENTIFYING YOUR INTERESTS - PART B

INSTRUCTIONS: *Select the **two** statements that you would enjoy doing the most from each group of eight. Write the corresponding numbers of these **two** statements in the boxes to the right of each group of eight.*

1. researching important historical events
2. achieving a high level of proficiency on a musical instrument or voice
3. learning how to invest in the stock market
4. solving mathematical problems
5. making a class presentation speaking in a language other than English
6. learning about scientific theories
7. helping to coach a sports team
8. sketching pictures

9. writing code for a new software application
10. writing a creative story
11. working as a volunteer to help others in your community
12. working with machinery or power tools
13. analyzing a dramatic performance
14. learning about ancient civilizations
15. experimenting with different techniques for painting a picture
16. starting your own business

17. performing on a musical instrument or voice before a large audience
18. conducting experiments in biology
19. learning about new advances in exercise techniques
20. helping as a teaching assistant in one of your classes
21. translating newspaper articles from one language to another
22. administering a website
23. studying the content and style of great literary works
24. graphing equations

> **INSTRUCTIONS:** *Select the two statements that you would enjoy doing the most from each group of eight. Write the corresponding numbers of these two statements in the boxes to the right of each group of eight.*

25. using a software program to design a house
26. practicing improvisation and role playing in a drama class
27. completing a project on urban planning
28. learning advertising techniques for marketing new products
29. researching a project on the life of a famous artist
30. employing exponential functions to model real world situations
31. researching the mechanics of human body movements
32. completing a project on an ecosystem

33. auditioning for a part in a local theatre presentation
34. writing an essay using a language other than your first language
35. installing security features for a home computer
36. writing articles for a magazine or newspaper
37. studying the psychology of human behavior
38. completing an electronics project
39. studying musical theory
40. researching different cultures

41. completing an accounting assignment
42. analyzing the painting techniques of famous works of art
43. conducting chemistry experiments
44. practicing a musical instrument or voice for at least 1 hour every day
45. completing a project related to nutrition
46. solving algebraic equations
47. reading a novel in a language other than your first language
48. editing a video

INSTRUCTIONS: *Select the two statements that you would enjoy doing the most from each group of eight. Write the corresponding numbers of these two statements in the boxes to the right of each group of eight.*

49. discussing books you have read
50. tutoring a student who has a learning problem
51. repairing an engine
52. researching a project on contemporary theatre
53. sculpting a face using clay
54. presenting a project on solutions to environmental problems
55. reading about the rights of employees in the workplace
56. solving problems related to financial applications

57. organizing and running a house league tournament
58. learning about quantum physics
59. learning the vocabulary of a language other than your first language
60. working as a volunteer in a local hospital
61. designing a website for a business
62. studying the works of famous authors such as Shakespeare
63. composing music
64. assisting in building a house

65. creating and presenting a dramatic short play
66. exploring different political systems
67. completing a project on factors that affect our economy
68. drawing or painting copies of famous works of art
69. exploring applications of compound interest to financial investments
70. researching the lives of famous composers
71. reading about advances in microbiology
72. studying the psychology of being a champion athlete

73. helping to build a broadcast studio
74. installing and configuring computer components
75. making a presentation to your class on a book you have read
76. learning the components of being an effective listener
77. interpreting someone speaking a foreign language you have learned
78. studying set designs for plays from different historical periods
79. completing a graphic design assignment using a computer
80. writing an essay on the causes of a major war

81. reading about people who have achieved great success in a business
82. completing a project on logarithmic functions
83. working as an instructor in a fitness club
84. completing a project on the human immune system
85. learning the grammatical rules of a foreign language
86. providing music lessons to younger students
87. setting up e-commerce capabilities on a business website
88. presenting a speech on a topic of your choice

89. assisting elderly people
90. completing a course in welding
91. analyzing a dramatic play
92. solving problems involving vectors in 2 + 3 dimensional space
93. reading about solutions to help resolve world hunger
94. experimenting with light and contrast in creating designs
95. learning about e-commerce trends
96. completing a project on living a healthy lifestyle

97. learning about molecular genetics
98. using a computer to arrange a musical selection
99. studying a short story written in another language you have learned
100. writing computer programs to drive devices such as robots
101. writing a fictional book
102. researching a project on the changing structure of families
103. installing mechanical devices
104. creating an original screenplay

Congratulations on finishing **PART B**.
*The next four pages will give you instructions
on how to interpret your results.
On these pages you will begin to see
how your interests relate to possible career choices.*

*"Where your interests meet the needs
of this world, there lies your vocation."*
Aristotle

A SUMMARY OF YOUR INTERESTS - PART A

SUBJECT AREA	QUESTION NUMBERS FROM PAGES 14 - 17								TOTALS
SOCIAL SCIENCE	1	14	27	40	53	66	79	92	
BUSINESS	2	15	28	41	54	67	80	93	
ART	3	16	29	42	55	68	81	94	
MATH-EMATICS	4	17	30	43	56	69	82	95	
RECREATION	5	18	31	44	57	70	83	96	
SCIENCE	6	19	32	45	58	71	84	97	
MUSIC	7	20	33	46	59	72	85	98	
LANGUAGES	8	21	34	47	60	73	86	99	
COMPUTERS	9	22	35	48	61	74	87	100	
ENGLISH	10	23	36	49	62	75	88	101	
SERVICE	11	24	37	50	63	76	89	102	
TECHNICAL	12	25	38	51	64	77	90	103	
DRAMATIC ARTS	13	26	39	52	65	78	91	104	

A SUMMARY OF YOUR INTERESTS - PART B

SUBJECT AREA	QUESTION NUMBERS FROM PAGES 18 - 22								TOTALS
SOCIAL SCIENCE	1	14	27	40	54	66	80	93	
BUSINESS	3	16	28	41	55	67	81	95	
ART	8	15	29	42	53	68	79	94	
MATHEMATICS	4	24	30	46	56	69	82	92	
RECREATION	7	19	31	45	57	72	83	96	
SCIENCE	6	18	32	43	58	71	84	97	
MUSIC	2	17	39	44	63	70	86	98	
LANGUAGES	5	21	34	47	59	77	85	99	
COMPUTERS	9	22	35	48	61	74	87	100	
ENGLISH	10	23	36	49	62	75	88	101	
SERVICE	11	20	37	50	60	76	89	102	
TECHNICAL	12	25	38	51	64	73	90	103	
DRAMATIC ARTS	13	26	33	52	65	78	91	104	

SUMMARIZING YOUR INTERESTS

INSTRUCTIONS: *On the following chart place your total scores from page 23 in Column A and your scores from page 24 in Column B. In Column C add your scores for each interest area from Columns A and B.*

INTEREST AREA	COLUMN A (from page 23)	COLUMN B (from page 24)	COLUMN C (from A + B)
SOCIAL SCIENCE			
BUSINESS			
ART			
MATHEMATICS			
RECREATION			
SCIENCE			
MUSIC			
LANGUAGES			
COMPUTERS			
ENGLISH			
SERVICE			
TECHNICAL			
DRAMATIC ARTS			

YOUR TOP THREE INTERESTS

On the above chart you can see the areas that you appear to have the strongest interest in by looking at your scores in Column C (NOTE: these are not necessarily the things that you do best. You will identify the things that you do best in the next chapter of this book).

INSTRUCTIONS: *In BOX 1 below, list your top three interest areas from the above chart (an extra space is provided in the event you have any ties).*

BOX 1

INTEREST AREA	SCORE

A FIRST LOOK AT POSSIBLE CAREER CHOICES

INSTRUCTIONS: *List your three highest interest areas from BOX 1 on the bottom of page 25 with your highest interest area going in BOX 2 below; your second highest interest area in BOX 3 below; and your third highest interest area in BOX 4 below.*

From the careers listed on pages 27 - 31, select 3 - 5 careers you think would be future possibilities for you from each of your highest three interest categories and write these careers in the appropriate boxes below. A sample box is provided to illustrate what you are to do.

SAMPLE BOX

If your highest interest score (from page 25) was "BUSINESS", you would go to the BUSINESS list of careers on page 27 and then select 3 - 5 careers that are future possibilities for you from this list and enter them in this box. So for example, your list might look like this:

entrepreneur, financial planner, investment analyst

YOUR HIGHEST INTEREST AREA =

BOX 2

YOUR SECOND HIGHEST INTEREST AREA =

BOX 3

YOUR THIRD HIGHEST INTEREST AREA =

BOX 4

ANTHROPOLOGIST	GEOLOGICAL TECHNICIAN	LIBRARIAN
ARCHAEOLOGIST	GOVERNMENT WORKER	MARKET RESEARCHER
ARCHIVIST	HISTORIAN	MINING SUPERVISOR
CHILD + YOUTH WORKER	HOTEL WORKER	MUSEUM EDUCATOR
COMMUNITY LEADER	HUMAN RESOURCES MANAGER	NEWS ANALYST
CONSERVATION OFFICER	HUMAN RIGHTS OFFICER	PARALEGAL
COUNSELOR	IMMIGRATION OFFICER	POLICY WRITER
COURT OFFICER	INFORMATION ANALYST	POLITICAL ORGANIZER
CURATOR	JOURNALIST	PSYCHOLOGIST
FAMILY SERVICES WORKER	LABOR RELATIONS OFFICER	REAL ESTATE SALES
FLIGHT ATTENDANT	LAND SURVEYOR	SOCIAL WORKER
FORESTRY PROFESSIONALS	LAND USE PLANNER	TEACHER
GEOGRAPHER	LAWYER	TOURISM WORKER

BUSINESS

ACCOUNT EXECUTIVE	CHIEF EXECUTIVE OFFICER	LAWYER
ACCOUNTANT	CLAIMS ADJUSTER	LEASING SERVICES
ACCOUNTS PAYABLE CLERK	COST ESTIMATOR	LOAN OFFICER
ACTUARY	CUSTOMER SERVICES	MARKETING ANALYST
ADMINISTRATIVE ASSISTANT	CUSTOMS BROKER	OFFICE ASSISTANT
ADMINISTRATIVE MANAGER	DATA ENTRY CLERK	PAYROLL OFFICER
ANALYST	ECONOMIST	RECEPTIONIST
APPRAISER	EMPLOYEE RELATIONS	RETAIL PERSONNEL
AUDITOR	ENTREPRENEUR	SALESPERSON
BANK WORKER	EXECUTIVE ASSISTANT	SECRETARY
BUDGET SUPERVISOR	FINANCIAL PLANNER	STORE MANAGER
BUYER	HUMAN RESOURCES MANAGER	TELEMARKETER
CASHIER	INVESTMENT ANALYST	WEB SPECIALIST

ART

ADVERTISING DESIGNER	COSMETICIAN	GRAPHIC ARTIST
ANIMATOR	CRAFTSPERSON	HAIRSTYLIST
ANTIQUE DEALER	CURATOR	ILLUSTRATOR
ANTIQUE RESTORER	DECORATOR	INTERIOR DESIGNER
ARCHITECT	DESIGN TECHNICIAN	LANDSCAPE ARCHITECT
ART DEALER	DISPLAY DESIGNER	PHOTO EDITOR
ARTIST	ESTHETICIAN	POTTER
ARTISAN	FASHION DESIGNER	SCULPTOR
ARTISTIC DIRECTOR	FILM EDITOR	SET DESIGNER
BAKER	FLORIST	TEACHER/INSTRUCTOR
CABINETMAKER	FREELANCER	WARDROBE SUPERVISOR
CAD TECHNOLOGIST	FURNITURE DESIGNER	WEBSITE ARTIST
CLOTHING DESIGNER	GAMES DESIGNER	WEBSITE DESIGNER

MATHEMATICS

ACCOUNTANT	CREDIT MANAGER	PHARMACIST
ACCOUNTNG CLERK	ENGINEER	PILOT
ACTUARY	ENGINEERING TECHNICIAN	PRODUCT DESIGNER
AGRICULTURAL PROFESSIONAL	FINANCIAL PLANNER	PRODUCT SUPPORT
ANALYST	INCOME TAX SPECIALIST	PURCHASING AGENT
ARCHITECT	INSURANCE BROKER	SALES REPRESENTATIVES
AUDITOR	INVESTMENT ANALYST	SCIENCE PROFESSIONAL
BANKING CLERK	LASER TECHNICIAN	SECURITIES TRADER
CASHIER	LOANS OFFICER	STATISTICIAN
CHEMIST	MARKET ANALYST	SYSTEMS CONTROLS
COMPUTER PROGRAMMER	MECHANIC	TEACHER/INSTRUCTOR
COMPUTER TECHNICIAN	MEDICAL TECHNICIAN	TECHNICIAN
COST ESTIMATOR	PAYROLL OFFICER	WEB ARCHITECT

RECREATION

ATHLETE	FLIGHT SERVICES	RECREATION PLANNER
ATHLETIC THERAPIST	FOOD SERVICES WORKER	RESORT STAFF
BANQUET STAFF	GUEST + HOTEL SERVICES	RESTAURANT STAFF
CHEF	KINESIOLOGIST	RETIREMENT COUNSELOR
CONVENTION WORKER	LANDSCAPE WORKER	RETIREMENT SERVICES
CORPORATE TRAVEL	LEISURE CONSULTANT	SALES PERSONNEL
DANCE THERAPIST	LIFESTYLE PLANNER	TICKET AGENT
DANCER	PARKS MANAGER	TOUR GUIDE
ENTERTAINER	PARKS WORKER	TOUR OPERATOR
EVENT MANAGEMENT	PHYSIOTHERAPIST	TOURISM COORDINATOR
EVENT STAFF	PHYSIOTHERAPIST AIDE	TRAVEL AGENT
FITNESS CONSULTANT	PRO ATHLETE	TRAVEL WRITER
FITNESS INSTRUCTOR	RECREATION DIRECTOR	WAITER/WAITRESS

SCIENCE

AGRICULTURAL EXPERT	DENTIST	MEDICAL ASSISTANT
ALTERNATE ENERGY EXPERT	DIETICIAN	MEDICAL SECRETARY
ANIMAL CARE TECHNICIAN	ENGINEER	NURSE
ANIMAL TECHNOLOGIST	FISHERIES PROFESSIONAL	NURSING ASSISTANT
AUDIOLOGIST	FORENSIC CHEMIST	NUTRITIONIST
BIOCHEMIST	FORESTRY PROFESSIONAL	OPTOMETRIST
BIOLOGIST	GENETICIST	PHARMACIST
BIOMEDICAL TECHNICIAN	GREENHOUSE MANAGER	PHYSICIAN
CHEMIST	HEALTH CARE AIDE	POLLUTION CONTROL
CHIROPRACTOR	HORTICULTURIST	RESPIRATORY TECHNICIAN
CHIROPRACTOR AIDE	LAB TECHNOLOGIST	VETERINARIAN
CLINICAL LEADER	LABORATORY TESTER	VETERINARIAN ASSISTANT
CONSERVATION OFFFICER	LANDSCAPE ARCHITECT	X-RAY TECHNICIAN

MUSIC

ACTOR	MULTIMEDIA SOUND TECH.	PERFORMING ARTIST
ANNOUNCER/BROADCASTER	MUSIC ARRANGER	PROFESSIONAL MUSICIAN
CHOREOGRAPHER	MUSIC COORDINATOR	PUBLICIST
COMPOSER	MUSIC COPYIST	RECORDING PRODUCER
CONDUCTOR	MUSIC CRITIC	RECORDING TECHNICIAN
DANCER	MUSIC DIRECTOR	SINGER
ENTERTAINER	MUSIC LIBRARIAN	SOUND EDITOR
ENTERTAINMENT ORGANIZER	MUSIC SALESPERSON	STAGE BAND MEMBER
EVENT STAFF	MUSIC THERAPIST	STAGE CREW
INSTRUCTOR/TEACHER	MUSIC VIDEO DIRECTOR	STUDIO MANAGER
INSTRUMENT REPAIRER	MUSICAL INSTRUMENT TUNER	TALENT SCOUT
INSTRUMENT SALESPERSON	MUSICAL THEATRE DIRECTOR	VIDEOGRAPHER
MULTIMEDIA PRODUCER	MUSICAL THEATRE STAFF	VIDEO DIRECTOR

LANGUAGES

ANNOUNCER/BROADCASTER	GOVERNMENT WORKER	PUBLIC RELATIONS
BUYER	HOTEL MANAGER	RECEPTIONIST
CAREGIVER	HOTEL SERVICES WORKER	RESORT STAFF
CASHIER	HUMAN RIGHTS OFFICER	RESTAURANT STAFF
CHAUFFEUR	IMMIGRATION OFFICER	SALESPERSON
CHIEF EXECUTIVE OFFICER	INTERNATIONAL RELATIONS	SPEECH PATHOLOGIST
COMMUNITY WORKER	INTERPRETER	TAXI DRIVER
CUSTOMER RELATIONS	JOURNALIST	TEACHER/INSTRUCTOR
CUSTOMER SERVICES	LAWYER	TOUR GUIDE
EMPLOYEE RELATONS	LIBRARIAN	TRANSLATOR
FAMILY SERVICES WORKER	LINGUIST	TRAVEL AGENT
FLIGHT ATTENDANT	NEWS ANALYST	TRAVEL + TOURISM
FLIGHT SERVICES	POLITICAL ORGANIZER	WAITER/WAITRESS

COMPUTERS

APPLICATIONS ENGINEER	ENGINEER	PRODUCT DEVELOPER
APPLICATIONS SUPPORT	ENTREPRENEUR	PROTOCOL SPECIALIST
BUSINESS INFO. ANALYST	FIREWALL TEST ENGINEER	SALES REPRESENTATIVE
BUSINESS SYSTEMS	GRAPHICS DESIGNER	SECURITY SPECIALIST
COMPUTER ANALYST	HARDWARE DESIGNER	SOFTWARE DEVELOPER
COMPUTER PROGRAMMER	HARDWARE INSTALLER	SOLUTION ARCHITECT
COMPUTER TECHNICIAN	HELP DESK SUPPORT	SYSTEMS ANALYST
CONFIGURATION MANAGER	INSTALLATION SERVICES	TECHNICAL WRITER
CUSTOMER ENGINEER	INTERNET SOLUTIONS TECH.	TEACHER/INSTRUCTOR
DATA ARCHITECT	MARKET RESEARCHER	TESTER
DATABASE ADMINISTRATOR	MASTER SCHEDULER	VIDEO/FILM EDITOR
E-BUSINESS CONSULTANT	MULTIMEDIA INTERFACE	WEBSITE ADMINISTRATOR
E-COMMERCE SPECIALIST	NETWORK ADMINISTRATOR	WEBSITE DESIGNER

ENGLISH		
ACTOR	EDITORIAL ASSISTANT	MARKETING ANALYST
ADMINISTRATOR	FILM CRITIC	MARKETING DIRECTOR
ADMINISTRATIVE AIDE	FILM DIRECTOR	NEWS EDITOR
ADVERTISING DIRECTOR	HISTORIAN	NOVELIST
ANNOUNCER/BROADCASTER	HUMAN RESOURCES MANAGER	PARALEGAL
ARCHIVIST	INSURANCE BROKER	PROOFREADER
AUTHOR	JOURNALIST	PUBLICIST
BOOK CRITIC	LAWYER	RECEPTIONIST
COMMUNICATIONS EXPERT	LEGISLATOR	SALESPERSON
CUSTOMER SERVICES	LIBRARIAN	SECRETARY
DATA ENTRY CLERK	LIBRARY ASSISTANT	SPEECH PATHOLOGIST
DISPATCHER	LINGUIST	TEACHER/INSTRUCTOR
EDITOR	MANAGER	WRITER

SERVICE		
AMBULANCE ATTENDANT	GERIATRIC WORKER	PARAMEDIC
BEREAVEMENT CONSELOR	HAIRSTYLIST	PERSONAL SUPPORT
CAREER ADVISOR	HOME HEALTH AIDE	WORKER
CASHIER	HOTEL SERVICES	PERSONNEL MANAGER
CHILD + YOUTH WORKER	HUMAN RESOURCES MANAGER	PHYSICIAN
CORRECTIONAL OFFICER	LABOR RELATIONS SPECIALIST	PHYSIOTHERAPIST
COUNSELOR	LAWYER	POLICE OFFICER
CUSTOMER SERVICES	LEGAL ASSISTANT	PSYCHIATRIST
DAY CARE WORKER	MASSAGE THERAPIST	RECREATON LEADER
DENTAL ASSISTANT	NANNY	REHABILITATION SERVICES
FIREFIGHTER	NURSE	SOCIAL WORKER
FLIGHT SERVICES	OCCUPATIONAL THERAPIST	SPECIAL NEEDS WORKER
FUNERAL SERVICES	PARALEGAL	TEACHER

TECHNICAL		
APPLIANCE SERVICE	CEMENT MASON	HEAVY EQUIPMENT
ARCHITECT	CLEANING SERVICES	INDUSTRIAL DESIGNER
ARCHITECTURAL TECH.	COMPUTER REPAIRS	INSTALLER
ASSEMBLER	CONTRACTOR	LANDSCAPE ARCHITECT
BACKHOE OPERATOR	CONSTRUCTION MANAGER	MACHINE DESIGNER
BOILERMAKER	DRILLER	MECHANIC
BRICKLAYER	DRIVERS, BUS + TRUCK	MILLWRIGHT
BUTCHER	ELECTRICIAN	MINING WORKER
CABINETMAKER	ENGINEER	PLUMBER
CABLE INSTALLER	ENGINEERING TECHNICIAN	PRODUCT DESIGNER
CAD TECHNOLOGIST	FIREFIGHTER	ROOFER
CARPENTER	FISHERMAN/WOMAN	SERVICE TECHNICIAN
CARPET CLEANER	FORKLIFT OPERATOR	WELDER

ACTOR	FILMMAKER	SALESPERSON
ACTING COACH	MAGICIAN	SCRIPT SUPERVISOR
ANNOUNCER/BROADCASTER	MAKE-UP ARTIST	SCRIPT WRITER
CAMERA OPERATOR	MAKE-UP CONSULTANT	SET DESIGNER
CHOREOGRAPHER	MODEL	SINGER
COLUMNIST	MUSEUM GUIDE	SPEECH WRITER
COMMUNICATIONS EXPERT	MUSICIAN	STAGE DIRECTOR
DANCE THERAPIST	PERFORMER	TALENT SCOUT
DANCER	PRODUCER	TEACHER/INSTRUCTOR
DIRECTOR	PROFESSIONAL SPEAKER	THEATRE STAFF
DRAMA COACH	PUBLICIST	WAITER/WAITRESS
ENTERTAINER	PUPPETEER	WARDROBE SUPERVISOR
FACILITIES MANAGER	RECORDING TECHNICIAN	WRITER

ADDITIONAL CAREERS

INSTRUCTIONS: *In this box write any occupations that you are interested in that were not already listed on pages 27 - 31.*

BOX 5

**Your greatest success
will come from building
on what you do best.**

IDENTIFYING YOUR ABILITIES

You are now ready to identify your abilities. In Chapter 1 you identified your interests. Interests are the things you enjoy doing, but they are not necessarily the things you do the best, although they can definitely be the things that you do best. The following story illustrates a student who had a strong interest but he didn't not have the ability to pursue this interest to turn it into his future career.

At the age of eighteen Jeff dreamed of being a professional baseball player. If anyone asked Jeff what he loved to do, he would say he loved to play baseball. Baseball was his strong interest. Unfortunately for Jeff, baseball was not the thing he did best. Jeff had poor coordination, was a slow runner, threw a baseball poorly, and rarely hit the ball. In other words, the thing that Jeff enjoyed doing the most was not the thing he was best at. His abilities did not match his interests. Even after hours of practice and years of trying, his abilities were not improving. What Jeff loved to do was play baseball, but what he did really well (with very little effort) was running a small business he had developed.

Identifying and understanding the things that you can do very well is another part of planning your future. You may find that what you do well is exactly the same as what you are interested in. On the other hand, you might discover that what you do well is not the same as the things you are most interested in. Later in this book you will learn how to combine your interests and abilities (whether they are the same or not) to plan your future.

Successful people focus on what they do best. When you are able to identify and understand the things that you love to do and do well, you will have taken a big step forward towards your future success. When your future education/training is based on pursuing your strengths (combining both your interests and abilities), you will

Successful people build on their strengths.

find your future education/training exciting. You will look forward to your classes each day because you are doing what you really want to do.

When you spend most of your time and energy doing what you do best and love to do, it will be easier for you to achieve success. To discover your abilities, ask yourself a few questions. What is something you can do better than most other people? What is something you do that doesn't seem like work for you? What is something that you do that brings compliments from others? Throughout this chapter you will be exploring answers to these questions.

Below, and on the next few pages, is a list of ability categories and a brief description of the school courses and interests that are associated with each one. The ability categories are given in alphabetical order. It is important to realize that the school subjects listed under each category may not all be offered at your high school. In some cases there may be subjects that you have studied that are not listed (if there is a school subject that you are strongly interested in, ask your parents or teachers which interest area that subject would best fit, and then add it to the appropriate category in this list). You may also notice that some school subjects may be listed under more than one ability category. As you read the description of each ability category, begin to think about which category best describes your abilities.

ART: this includes courses and interests such as art, visual arts, graphic design, photography, printmaking, set design, retail design, drawing, sketching, illustration, painting, sculpting, pottery making, architecture and interior design.

BUSINESS: this includes courses and interests such as business studies, communication studies, group dynamics, workplace ethics, financial management, investment strategies, accounting, entrepreneurship studies, marketing, economics, management theory, management fundamentals, information technology, e-business, and business law.

COMPUTERS: this includes courses and interests such as computers + information science, computer engineering, programming, software development, website development, website administration, designing computer components, e-business, constructing systems that use computer programs to interact with hardware and diagnosing hardware and software problems.

DRAMATIC ARTS: this includes courses and interests such as the exploration of dramatic forms and techniques, performing and analyzing drama, improvisation, role playing, acting, producing dramatic works, interpreting dramatic literature, directing theatrical productions and media studies.

ENGLISH: this includes courses and interests such as English studies, language arts, creative writing, persuasive writing, communication studies, analytical reading, communication skills, media studies, study of poetry, study of short stories, journalism, study of the works of famous authors and writing literary essays.

LANGUAGES: this includes courses and interests such as the study of a language other than your first language (defined here as a foreign language), oral communication of a foreign language, reading and writing a foreign language, study of customs associated with a foreign language, translating any form of communication from one language to another and studying literary + media works in a foreign language.

MATHEMATICS: this includes courses and interests such as mathematics, mathematical theories and related problem solving, algebra, geometry, trigonometry, graphing, accounting, functions, calculus and information management.

MUSIC: this includes courses and interests such as piano, voice, musical instrumentation, music theory, study of famous composers, arranging musical works, performing, analyzing music, recording + production techniques, study of music styles throughout various historical periods, practicing technical exercises and repertoire pieces, composing, studying software related to creating music, and conducting techniques.

RECREATION: this includes courses and interests such as healthy active living, physical education, exercise techniques, sports, fitness, health, lifestyle choices, athletic competitions, organizing tournaments, movement principles, kinesiology, sports administration and recreation.

Discover what you love to do and focus on taking further education and/or training in this area.

SCIENCE: this includes courses and interests such as scientific inquiry, biology, chemistry, physics, scientific theories, environment, ecosystems, scientific experimentation, genetics and scientific research.

SERVICE: this includes courses and interests such as volunteer work in the community or school, helping others, psychology, sociology, parenting, social work, medical studies, injury management, health care, teaching and counseling.

SOCIAL SCIENCE: this includes courses and interests such as history, geography, politics, humanities, parenting, world religions, family studies, environment, psychology, sociology, anthropology and archaeology.

TECHNICAL: this includes courses and interests such as engine repair/maintenance, vehicle repair/maintenance, working with machinery or power tools, carpentry, electrical, woodworking, construction, architecture, plumbing, instrumentation design, structural analysis and installation services.

OTHER: (list any other subject areas here that you have studied that were not already listed on pages 34 - 36)

IDENTIFYING YOUR TOP ABILITIES

INSTRUCTIONS: *In BOX 6 below, list your top 3 high school ability categories from pages 34 - 36 (including any subjects that you added to this list) in order of strength for you. The list of ability categories is also provided on the left hand side of this page for your convenience.*

The number one ability category that you write below will be the area that describes the things you are best at doing. The second ability category that you write will be your next best area and so on.

If you are having difficulty with this task it might be useful for you to talk to a teacher or counselor. In addition, your past and present report card marks may provide some indication of your ability in each subject areas.

ART

BUSINESS

COMPUTERS

DRAMATIC ARTS

ENGLISH

LANGUAGES

MATHEMATICS

MUSIC

RECREATION

SCIENCE

SERVICE

SOCIAL SCIENCES

TECHNICAL

OTHER

PRIORITIZING MY ABILITY CATEGORIES

My top three abilities

1. . . . .

2. . . . .

3. . . . .

BOX 6

INSTRUCTIONS: In BOX 7 below, write the five careers from BOXES 2, 3, and 4 on page 26 and any other occupations from BOX 5 at the bottom of page 31 that could be possible future careers for you.

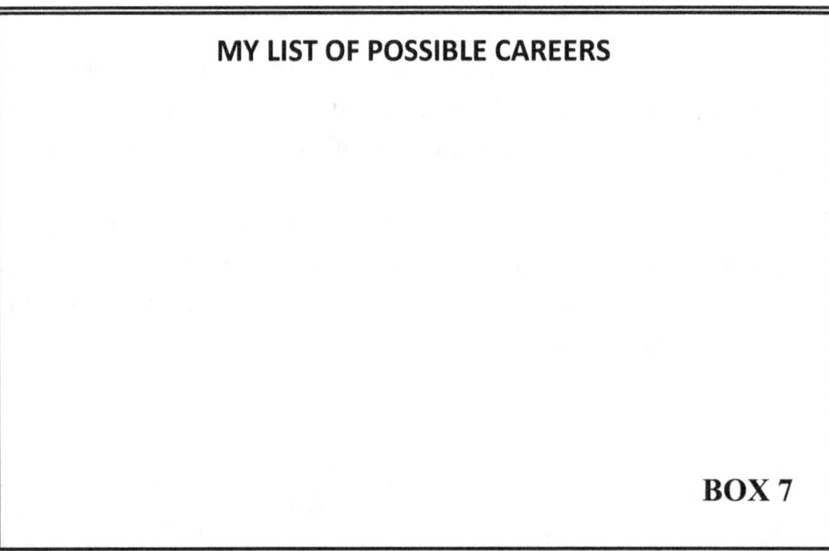

INSTRUCTIONS: *The occupations that you listed above (in BOX 7) were chosen by you based on your interests. On page 37, IN BOX 6, you identified your top 3 ability areas at school. Circle any (or even all) careers in BOX 7 above that have the strongest relationship to your best 3 ability areas in school (from BOX 6).*

In other words, circle any careers in BOX 7 above that depend on you doing well in one or more of your top 3 subject areas from BOX 6 on page 37. If you are having any difficulties completing this, ask your teacher/counselor/parents for help.

At this point, the careers you have circled above in BOX 7 appear to be the ones that best match both your interests and abilities. You might find it useful to show this list to your parents, teacher, or counsellor. Next, you have the opportunity to identify your values and look at how these also affect your future plans.

A REVIEW OF WHAT YOU HAVE LEARNED SO FAR

At the beginning of this book it was stressed that successful people build on their strengths. As a result, one of the best approaches to planning your future after high school is to begin by identifying your strengths and then identify career/educational/training possibilities that best match these strengths.

In the first chapter of this book you identified your interests by completing an interest survey. Once you had identified your interests, you were able to select some careers that best matched your interests.

In the second chapter, you explored your abilities. One way to identify some of your abilities is to consider which subjects in school you are best at doing. While this approach has the problem of not necessarily considering all your possible abilities, it can at least you give you an indication of some of the things you do well (especially as they relate to school success).

As you plan your future, it makes sense to choose a program at a college, university, or some other form of training or education, that best matches your interests and abilities.

BOX 6 on page 38 summarizes your results so far in this book. Hopefully you are now able to better identify your interests and abilities which it's possible you already knew. If so, your work so far may have confirmed what you already knew about yourself. If your results provide a new understanding of yourself, then this can hopefully help you to consider an appropriate path for your future.

From my experience in counseling high school students, I found that about 2/3 of students did not know what future career they wanted to pursue. If you are in that situation, an approach that you might want to consider is choosing a educational/training program after high school that best matches your interests and abilities. This way you are still building on your strengths, and at some later time (after high school) you will begin to better understand some of the careers that could result from your further education/training. It is okay not to know which future career you would like to pursue when you are in high school.

Your values are your personal success compass.

IDENTIFYING YOUR VALUES

Why Are Values Important To Consider In Planning Your Future?

To a very large degree your values will determine your satisfaction with whatever educational or training program you pursue after high school. What you value helps to create meaning in your life. For you to live your life to the fullest, it is important that your goals reflect your values. Your values are like a compass giving you direction. When your future planning follows the direction of your internal compass, as represented by your values, you will be enthusiastic and positive about whatever you are doing.

Mike graduated from high school with a desire to make a lot of money. He trained as a real estate agent. With strong communication skills and a passion to be successful, Mike was soon making the kind of money he had dreamed about. He bought an expensive condo, a great car, the best clothing and always had the money to do whatever he wanted. Unfortunately, though, Mike was not happy. Being a very successful real estate agent was not satisfying for him.

You will find personal satisfaction in your future career if it builds on your strengths and aligns with your values.

As Mike began to explore what was happening in his life, he thought about his past. In high school, Mike often volunteered with local community agencies to help kids who were experiencing problems. He always found great satisfaction in doing this. Helping others, especially children, was a core value for Mike. Although he hadn't recognized it at the time, this value was stronger for him than his desire to make a great deal of money. By ignoring this value, he had become unhappy even though he was very successful in his job.

Mike realized he could begin to do some volunteer work again, or use some of his money to help others, or he could even change careers. In Mike's situation, he gave up his lucrative career in real estate and went back to college to complete training to become a youth counselor.

After a few years of college, Mike began a new career in working with children. Although he would not likely earn as much money as he would have if he had remained in real estate, he found he was much happier working with kids.

What then is a value? A dictionary would define a value as:

- something of importance
- what something is worth
- the usefulness of something
- something you hold dear to you
- something you cherish
- something you regard highly and respect

A thesaurus would use some of the following words to describe value:

- worth, benefit, advantage
- importance, merit, significance
- usefulness, worthiness

As you begin to think of your values, ask yourself the following questions:

1. What is really important to you?

2) What is something you cherish about yourself?

3) What do you feel passionate about?

As you go through life, all the decisions that you make will be impacted by your values. When you make decisions that match your values, you will feel satisfied even if you face obstacles in what you are doing. If you make decisions that do not align with your values you may find yourself unhappy even though like Mike on the previous page you have achieved your initial goals.

When you know what is most important to you, your decisions become easier. You will find it easier to plan your future after high school when you are able to identify your core values.

The following provides a list of some possible values (and a brief description of each value). These values are given in the context of what you would be looking for in a future career.

Read the list of values on the next few pages, and begin to think about which of these values are most important to you. Later, you will be asked to select the 5 values that are most important to you.

ADVANCEMENT: you would like the opportunity to rise or be promoted to increasing levels of expertise, management or leadership within a company or organization.

CHALLENGE: you would like a future career that offers challenges for you each day. This is a job where you will need to constantly keep learning in order to be able to handle new projects that you are involved in each day.

COMPETITIVE: you would like a career where you are competing against others as part of your job. You enjoy the prospect of constantly trying to be the best in comparison to others.

CREATIVE EXPRESSION: you would like a career that offers an opportunity for you to be very creative. This would tend to be a job where you could best employ your artistic talents or be inventive.

ENTREPRENEURIAL: you would like a career that offers you the opportunity to do things your way (preferably to start your own business). You tend to enjoy taking risks and you are very good at promoting what you do.

FOLLOWER: you would like a career where someone tells you each day exactly what you have to do and how to do it. Your job would be to primarily follow instructions rather than create new ways of doing things.

Taking your first step in the right direction is more important than taking many steps going the wrong way.

HELP OTHERS: you would like a career where you are given the opportunity to make a difference in the lives of others.

HIGH EARNINGS: you would like a career where you have the opportunity to make a lot of money.

INDEPENDENCE: you would like a career where you have the freedom to choose when and how you want to work. This job would give you the flexibility to choose what you want to do each day.

KNOWLEDGE: you would like a career where you are constantly learning. Your job allows you to work in research and the development of new ideas and possibilities.

LEADERSHIP: you would like a career where you have the opportunity to be a leader. You like to influence others and be in charge.

PHYSICAL CHALLENGE: you would like a career where there is a strong physical component to what you do each day.

PRACTICAL: you would like a career where what you do each day is very practical and at the end of the day you can actually see something concrete that you have made, developed or designed.

PRECISE: you would like a career where your work depends on attention to detail.

PRESTIGE: you would like a career where you feel the job is looked upon by others as being prestigious giving you more status in the eyes of yourself and others.

PROBLEM SOLVING: you would like a career where each day there are problems and challenges to solve or resolve.

PUBLIC CONTACT: you would like a career that offers you the opportunity to meet new people each day such as customers and/or clients.

RECOGNITION: you would like a career where you receive recognition and/or respect from others, whether it is from strangers, or from the people you work with.

SERVICE: you would like a career where you assist other people in getting what they want and/or need.

SPIRITUALITY: you would like a career where you work each day with people who have the same spiritual beliefs as you or where you have the opportunity to share your spiritual beliefs with others.

STRUCTURE: you would like a career where there is a set structure and predictability to what you do each day. You tend not to like change.

TEAMWORK: you would like a career where you are often working as part of a team with other people. You like to share ideas with others and work together on projects or assignments.

VARIETY: you would like a career where there is constant variety in what you do each day. You look forward to doing something different each day.

WORK-LIFE BALANCE: you would like a career that provides an opportunity to balance your time with family, hobbies, or other interests with the time necessary to work in your job.

WORLD BETTERMENT: you would like a career where you have the opportunity to make this world a better place to live.

OTHER: perhaps there is a value that is important to you that has not been listed above. If so, write this value or these values below.

While it important to consider your values as you plan your future, it is also important to realize that some of your values may change as you get older (as can your interests as well). For example, right now you might value a career where you can do a lot of traveling, but some day if you have children you might not want to travel as much. Similarly right now you might want a career that is a lot of fun even if you are not making very much money, but this value can change once you purchase a car and/or a house, or begin to have other expenses that require you to make more money.

The values that are most important to you are not necessarily the ones that are most important to others. This, along with your own unique interests and abilities, is why you should make your own decisions for your future rather than following what your friends are doing.

Choose your own career path, otherwise someone else might choose the wrong one for you. Yes, it is important to get feedback from your family, teachers and friends, but ultimately it is a choice that you will have to make for yourself.

> *"When your values are clear to you, making decisions is easier."*
> Roy D. Disney

IDENTIFYING YOUR CORE VALUES

INSTRUCTIONS: *On the chart below (BOX 8), identify your top five values from pages 43 - 45 (including any that you wrote yourself on the page 45). It might be helpful for you to read all the values on these pages once again to familiarize yourself with what each of them means. In fact, most people will have to re-read the list several times in order to identify their top five values.*

In identifying your top five values, you do <u>not</u> have to place them in priority order - simply write them in any order on the chart below.

Remember, you are selecting the values that are most important to you, not the ones you think others want you to list.

advancement

challenge

competitive

creative expression

entrepreneurial

follower

help others

high earnings

independence

knowledge

leadership

physical challenge

practical

precise

prestige

problem solving

public contact

recognition

service

spirituality

structure

teamwork

variety

work-life balance

world betterment

other

THE FIVE VALUES THAT ARE MOST IMPORTANT TO ME

1. . . . .

2. . . . .

3. . . . .

4. . . . .

5. . . . .

BOX 8

INSTRUCTIONS: *In BOX 9 below, list any careers that you circled in BOX 7 on page 38.*

CAREERS I AM INTERESTED IN

BOX 9

INSTRUCTIONS: *The careers that you listed above (in BOX 9) were chosen by you based on your interests and abilities. On page 47 you identified your top 5 values. Circle any (or even all) careers in BOX 9 above that have the strongest relationship to most, or even all, of your top five values.*

In other words, circle any careers in BOX 9 above that would best fulfill or satisfy the values that are most important to you. For instance, if you valued "high earnings", which of the above careers would bring you high earnings? If you valued "challenge", which of the above careers would bring challenges your way?

If you are having any difficulties completing this, ask your teacher/counselor/ parents for help.

MY TOP 3 CAREER CHOICES

INSTRUCTIONS: *On page 48, you identified a list of your top careers (based on your interests and abilities). Next, you circled any occupations in this list that also best matched your values. The careers that you circled would appear to be the ones that best match your interests, abilities, and values.*

In BOX 10 below, list the top 2 - 3 careers that would seem to best match your interests, abilities, and values (from BOX 9 on page 48)

MY TOP 2 - 3 CAREER CHOICES
(based on my interests, abilities, and values)

BOX 10

The next chapter will provide a summary of what you have learned so far in this book. It should help you to further clarify possible choices for your future although as it has been previously stated it is okay if you don't know the exact career you want to pursue.

As you think about your future, keep in mind that it is not unusual for students to change their career choice as they complete further education or training after high school. We live in a rapidly changing world where new careers often appear each year. The key in preparing for a changing world (and changing job market) is to continue to build on your strengths. When your studies and/or training best match your interests, abilities, and values, you will be more successful even if you find yourself pursuing a future career that you didn't even know that it existed when you were in high school.

The final two chapters can help you to better set goals for your future based on what you have learned so far in this book.

**Success and happiness
will follow you
when your future plans
are an extension
of who you are.**

SETTING A PLAN FOR YOUR FUTURE

This chapter can help you to establish a plan for your future after high school. As has been stated throughout this book, your best plan will build on your strengths. Some readers may have a clear vision of a future plan while others may still be unclear. Regardless, it is important for you to realize that many students successfully plan their future without knowing the exact occupation they want to someday pursue. As suggested in the last chapter, after you better understand your strengths (your interests, abilities, and values), the next step is to choose an educational or training program after you graduate from high school that best matches these strengths. Your actual career choice can come later if you aren't sure right now what you want to do.

One of the best ways to help ensure that you have a successful future is to focus right now on being successful in high school. If you establish strong work habits and develop a positive attitude, your future will generally be more successful even if you are unclear of what you want to someday do in terms of a career or even your education/training after high school.

The best way to plan for your future is often to focus right now on being successful in high school.

"By failing to prepare, you are preparing to fail."
Benjamin Franklin

"You have to believe in yourself when no one else does. That's what makes a winner."
Venus Williams
(Olympic gold medalist and tennis champion)

INSTRUCTIONS: *In BOX 11 write your top three interests from BOX 1 on page 25. In BOX 12 write your top three abilities from BOX 6 on page 37. In BOX 13 write your top three values from BOX 7 on page 47.*

This provides a summary of the strengths that you have identified for yourself in this book.

<table>
<tr><td>

MY TOP 3 INTERESTS

1.

2.

3.

(from page 25)   **BOX 11**

</td><td>

MY TOP 3 ABILITIES

1.

2.

3.

(from page 37)   **BOX 12**

</td></tr>
</table>

MY TOP 3 VALUES

1.

2.

3.

(from page 47)   **BOX 13**

INSTRUCTIONS: *In BOX 14 below, write 2 - 3 careers that are of the strongest interest to you. These careers should come from BOX 10 on page 49.*

MY TOP THREE CAREER POSSIBILITIES

1.

2.

3.

BOX 14

It is possible that you might plan for a future career, but unforeseen circumstances (such as a changing job market or not being accepted into the college/university program that you want to enter) might prevent you from successfully achieving this career. When this happens it can be beneficial for you to be aware of careers that are related to your main career choice. You might go in a slightly different direction while still choosing an occupation based on your strengths.

INSTRUCTIONS: *On the following chart, write your number one career choice (from BOX 14 on page 52) in the circle in the middle of the chart. Next, write down all the careers that you can think of that are related to this career. For example, if you wrote "doctor" in the middle circle some "related careers" might be nurse, medical supplies salesperson, x-ray technician, medical researcher, and so on. It might be useful to you to have other students work with you on this assignment.*

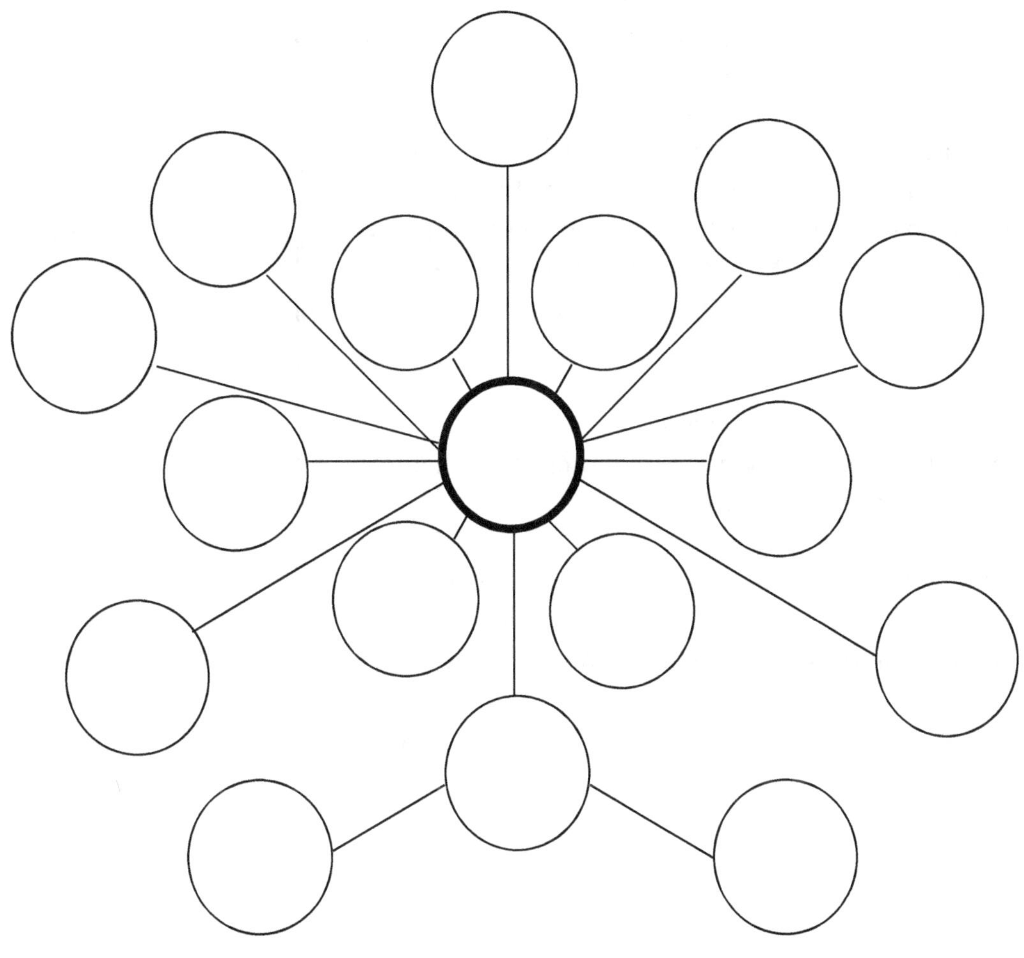

A FUTURE PLAN FOR YOU

As you complete the next few pages, it is strongly recommended that you work with a teacher/counselor and/or your parents to give you feedback on the appropriateness of your plans.

Whatever your plans for after high school, one immediate goal should be to graduate from high school. A high school diploma is an important achievement which is often a basic requirement for further education/training and is often a basic requirement for many entry-level jobs. Even if you are uncertain of your future plans you can help to create a better future by focusing on being the best student you can be right now in high school. Page 55 provides an opportunity to summarize the courses you have already completed in high school and then identify the courses (and any other requirements) that you will need to complete to graduate from high school.

For some students, focusing on doing well in high school (which includes strong attendance and working hard in a positive manner to learn as much as possible) may be your best immediate plan to lay the foundation for a successful future, even if you are unsure of your future plans.

INSTRUCTIONS (after you complete page 55):
If you are planning to enter the workforce directly from high school, you should complete pages 56.

If you are planning on furthering your education/training after high school by attending a college/university or some other educational or career training institution, you should complete page 57.

The best way to get what you want is to have a clear picture of what it is that you want.

MY HIGH SCHOOL GRADUATION REQUIREMENTS

1. The number of subjects (credits) that are required at my high school in order to achieve a high school graduation diploma is . . .

2. So far, I have completed . . . . credits.

3. The following are the mandatory (required) courses (and any other requirements) I still need to complete in order to graduate from high school . . .

4. During my remaining time in high school I could best prepare for my future after high school by . . .

A PLAN FOR ENTERING THE WORKFORCE

1. An occupation I would like to enter after I complete high school is (from BOX 14 on page 52 or from the Related Careers Activity on page 53) . . .

2. I believe I would be successful in this job because . . .

3. Two websites I could use to help me find companies who are hiring for this job are . . .

4. After looking at the websites I identified in question #3, some companies who are currently hiring for this job are . . .

5. After looking at the job advertisements from the websites I identified in question #3, some of the things (such as education, skills, and/or personal traits) that companies are looking for in hiring for this occupation are . . .

1. From BOX 14 on page 52 (or from the "Related Careers" activity on page 53), my top career choice at this time is . . .

2. After I graduate from high school, an educational or training program I could enrol in to help me get the qualifications for this career is . . .

3. The websites for two or three colleges or universities (or other educational/ training institutions) that I could attend to study the program I identified in question #2 are . . .

4. In order to get accepted into the above colleges, universities, or other educational/training institutions, I would have to complete the following courses in high school . . .

5. In addition to successfully completing the courses I identified in #4 above, in order to get accepted into the colleges, universities, or other educational/training institutions, I would have to . . .

If you knew that you could achieve your dreams, what would you do with your life?

ACHIEVING YOUR GOALS

Learning how to set and achieve your goals is an important part of being successful. You may have great dreams for your future, but unless you set realistic goals for achieving them and unless you actually take action towards achieving your dreams, then unfortunately they will just remain as dreams.

There are a few key components to consider in achieving your goals. These are:

1. Identify what you want to achieve. In other words, what are your goals? Once you have identified your goals, you should write them down.

2. Keep a clear picture in your mind of what you want to achieve. Some successful people have found it very useful to prepare a "vision chart" where they cut pictures from magazines that illustrate how they want their future to look, and then glued these pictures onto a sheet of paper to remind them of their goals. You could also set a vision chart as a screensaver on your laptop or tablet.

To maintain your complete focus on achieving your goals is the secret of success.

3. Prepare a step-by-step plan for achieving your goals. This plan should be written down and referred to every day. Some people find it helpful to also write down a motivational quote to help them stay inspired to achieve their dreams. This chapter can help you to prepare a step-by-step plan as well as providing some inspirational quotes.

4. Constantly monitor your plan, and when necessary revise any steps in your plan if this is going to help you to be more successful in achieving your goals.

5. Reward yourself every time you complete a step in your plan.

TIPS ON ACHIEVING YOUR GOALS

1. Always write your goals down.
A goal not written down is not a goal.

2. Spend the greatest amount of your time each day on the things
that will have the greatest impact on achieving your goals.

3. List all the ways both you and others will benefit
when you achieve your goals.

4. Keep a clear vision in your mind that shows you
having already successfully completed your goals.

5. Goals are best achieved when you break them into small,
sequential steps that have appropriate and definite timelines.

6. When you encounter an obstacle,
look for a new path that leads to your desired goal.

7. You can create your own good luck through hard work,
dedication to your goals, and believing you will be successful.

8. The biggest rewards in life are often when you move outside
your own comfort zone. Overcoming your fears
and taking risks often lead to the greatest successes.

9. The best way to kill an opportunity is to avoid taking it.
As you focus on your goals, always keep an open mind
for flexible ways of achieving them.

10. After writing down a goal, never leave it without
first taking some positive action towards completing it.

A ONE YEAR PLAN FOR ME

1. A major goal for me during the next year is . . .

2. In order for me to achieve this goal, three things I will have to accomplish during this year are . . .

   i)

   ii)

   iii)

3. A date for completing #2 - (i) is

4. A date for completing #2 - (ii) is

5. A date for completing #2 - (iii) is

6. Someone I can talk to about achieving my goals is . . .

7. I will benefit from achieving the goal I identified in #1 by . . .

1. A major goal I would like to accomplish within the next 3 - 5 years is . . .

2. In order for me to achieve this goal, up to 10 things (or steps) that I will have to complete along the way are . . .

i)

ii)

iii)

iv)

v)

vi)

vii)

viii)

ix)

x)

A 3 - 5 YEAR PLAN FOR ME

3. Place each of the 10 steps/things you identified in #2 on the left hand side of the following timeline and then write a specific date on the right hand side as to when you expect to have each step/thing completed

My Goal:

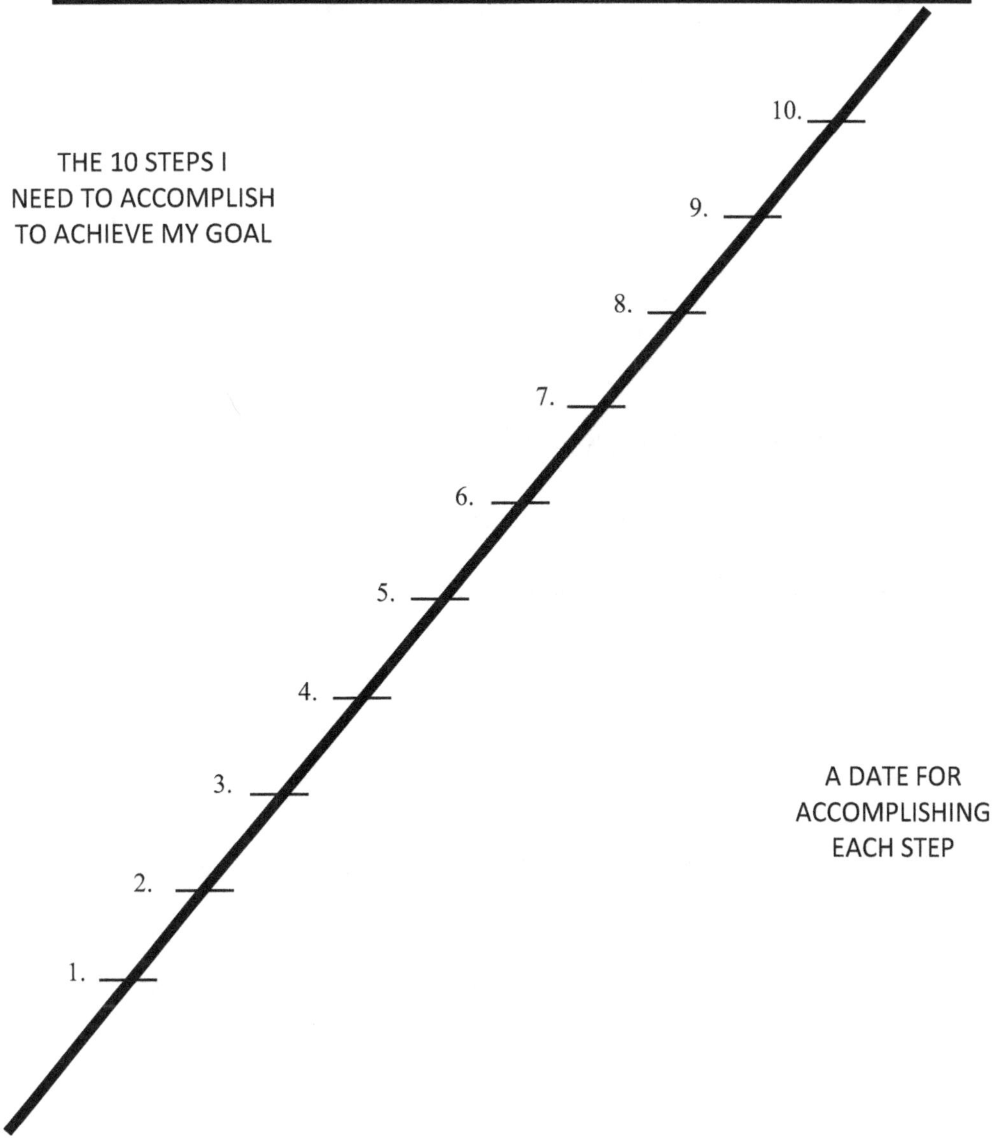
10.
9.
8.
7.
6.
5.
4.
3.
2.
1.
THE 10 STEPS I NEED TO ACCOMPLISH TO ACHIEVE MY GOAL
A DATE FOR ACCOMPLISHING EACH STEP

4. A quote that I could keep in mind to help me achieve my future goals is . . .

5. Three tips I could keep in mind to help me achieve my goals are . . .

    i)

    ii)

    iii)

6. Someone I can talk to about achieving my goal is . . .

7. I will benefit from achieving the goal I identified in #1 by . . .

QUOTES RELATED TO SUCCESS

"Success is not the key to happiness. Happiness is the key to success.
If you love what you are doing, you will be successful."
Albert Schweitzer

"I never dreamed about success. I worked for it."
Estee Lauder

"I know the price of success: determination, hard work,
and a devotion to the things you want to see happen."
F. L . Wright

"You have to do what you dream of doing,
even when you're afraid."
Arianna Huffington

"Success consists of going from failure to failure without loss of enthusiasm."
Winston Churchill

"The greatest barrier to success is the fear of failure."
Sven Goran Erikson

"Success means having the courage, the determination,
and the will to become the person you believe you were meant to be."
G. Sheehan

"Motivation will almost always beat mere talent."
N. R. Augustine

"Nothing will ever be attempted if all possible objections must first be overcome."
S. Johnson

"Many of life's failures are people who did not realize
how close they were to success when they gave up."
Thomas Edison

"To tend unfailingly, unflinchingly,
towards a goal is the secret of success."
Anna Pavlova

TIPS ON ACHIEVING SUCCESS

1. Success is sometimes going from failure to failure without losing enthusiasm for what you really want to achieve.

2. There is no such thing as failure. Everything that you do is a lesson helping you to learn how to be more successful achieving your goals.

3. If you want to change your life, begin with changing yourself.

4. Excuses and blame are obstacles that can get in the way of being successful. The critical factor in becoming successful is to take 100% responsibility for your life.

5. The fastest way to achieve success is to find someone who is already successful in what you want to accomplish and then model what they do. If possible, ask this person if he/she can be a mentor for you.

6. Winners have developed certain habits. When your life is based on these same habits, you too will become a winner.

7. Keep a constant focus on what you want as though you have already achieved it.

8. Surround yourself with successful people.

9. You will achieve your greatest success when what you do every day is aligned with your interests, your abilities and your values.

10. No one achieves their dreams without being determined.

SOME FINAL THOUGHTS TO HELP YOU ACHIEVE YOUR DREAMS

There have been four underlying themes throughout this book to help you achieve your dreams. These four themes are:

1) You Are Responsible For Your Future

2) Build Your Future On Your Strengths

3) Visualize Yourself Being Successful

4) Take action!

1) You Are Responsible For Your Future

If you don't have a plan for your future, then someone else is going to make one for you whether it is best for you or not. Some people go through their lives always blaming others for their lack of success. Successful people go through their lives taking responsibility for whatever comes their way. If you find that you are not achieving the success that you would like, then you may need to do things a different way. Change your habits and you can change your outcomes. Successful people develop habits that contribute to being successful. To learn these habits, find someone who is successful and copy what they do.

You may not always be able to change what is happening around you, but you can change yourself. The quality of your life is your choice. This means throwing away any excuses for not being successful. Whenever things don't turn out as you planned, ask yourself, "How can I do it differently next time to get the results that I want?"

Identify your future goals and then organize all your activities around achieving them.

2) Build Your Future On Your Strengths

We all have an inner guidance system. When your goals are in harmony with your interests, abilities, and values you will find the greatest joy and success in all that you do. When you focus your time and energy doing the things you really love and are good at, you will eventually receive huge rewards.

Every day, think about what it is that you do really well. Constantly build on your strengths. When your future goals are based on your loves, you will achieve your greatest results. To achieve your goals, you may have to say "NO" when others try to steer you in another direction. The difference between success and failure for most people is simply a matter of focus. Take a little time throughout each day to ensure you are focusing on achieving YOUR goals.

3) Visualize Yourself Being Successful

Whatever you think about the most, you will tend to become. Start each day by reading your goals. Keep a clear picture of your dreams in your mind. When you do this, your subconscious will help you work towards accomplishing these dreams. Constantly visualize yourself as being successful in achieving your dreams. Whenever you find yourself thinking about failure, STOP and change your thinking.

Whatever you believe is true will lead you towards that reality. Focus on where you want to go, not your fears. Create goals that you get excited about.

4) Take Action!

Always remember that a dream without action will always still just be a dream. Take action every day towards achieving your dreams, even if it's only some small step. Ask yourself often whether what you are spending most of your time doing is contributing directly to achieving your future goals.

The smallest steps in the right direction can result in huge accomplishments.

ISBN 9781791996819

ISBN 9781791612139

Other Books by Brian Harris

ISBN 9781533408105

About the Author

Brian Harris is an award-winning teacher/counselor and best-selling author. He has extensive experience in working with children of all ages in elementary schools, high schools, colleges and universities. He has also achieved the designation of International Professional Speaker. He has extensive experience in the field of educational/career planning as well as self-esteem.

Brian lives in Ontario, Canada, with his wife and daughters. In addition to writing, Brian is a part-time lecturer in counseling at Queen's University. He is also an accomplished artist (www.bcharris.com).

Brian enjoys family trips and is an avid canoeist and scuba diver.

Additional information about Brian can be found at
www.cgscommunications.com